Let's Get the Ball Rolling!

Easy-to-Remember English Idioms Language Book for Kids

Children's ESL Books

In this book, we're going to talk about common and easy-to-remember English idioms. So, let's get right to it!

WHAT IS AN IDIOM?

An idiom is a phrase with a meaning that isn't completely clear from the actual words in the phrase. For example, let's say you use the phrase, "it's raining cats and dogs." You don't really mean that cats and dogs are falling from the sky, you just mean that it's pouring rain.

Sometimes historians know exactly where an idiom came from, but frequently there are lots of theories about the history of an idiom. No matter where an idiom started, it stuck in people's minds, became part of the English language, and continued to be used for centuries. Many idioms come from events in history, social status, sports activities, or religion.

IT'S RAINING
CATS AND
DOGS.

COMMON IDIOM 1

Get the ball rolling

WHAT DOES IT MEAN?

It means that you're going to start something. It's believed that this phrase was started in the late 1700s from different types of sports where a ball had to be put in motion for the sport to begin.

A SAMPLE SENTENCE
"Let's get the ball rolling," said the hostess at the start of the party.

COMMON IDIOM 2

Woke up or got up on the
wrong side of the bed

WHAT DOES IT MEAN?

It means that someone is in a bad or cranky mood. In ancient times, there was a superstition that said if you put your left foot down on the floor first, then it was bad luck. The phrase was used in some plays written in the 17th century. By the 1800s, it was connected more with being in a bad mood than having bad luck.

A SAMPLE SENTENCE

He was so grouchy that I could tell he woke up on the wrong side of the bed.

COMMON IDIOM 3
Let the cat out of the bag

WHAT DOES IT MEAN?

It means that you told a secret that you weren't supposed to tell. No one knows for sure where the phrase came from, but a copy of The London Magazine published in 1760 had a review of a book where the reviewer said that he wished a particular author hadn't "let the cat out of the bag."

Another even earlier theory is that sneaky farmers would commit fraud by substituting cats instead of piglets that were sold at the market. This theory dates back to the 16th century. Of course, if someone opened the bag, the cat would run out and no one would be having pork chops for dinner.

A SAMPLE SENTENCE

The party was supposed to be a surprise, but her sister let the cat out of the bag.

COMMON IDIOM 4
Butter someone up

WHAT DOES IT MEAN?

It means to flatter them too much to gain favor from them. In India in ancient times people would throw balls of clarified butter at sculptures of their gods. This ceremony was done so the gods would forgive them and give them good fortune.

A SAMPLE SENTENCE

She tried to compliment her mother-in-law to butter her up.

COMMON IDIOM 5

Bite the bullet

WHAT DOES IT MEAN?

It means that you have to endure something that isn't comfortable or is painful. Before it was common to give people anesthetic before surgery, patients would sometimes bite down on a bullet in order to endure the pain of an operation.

A SAMPLE SENTENCE

He didn't feel like doing his math homework, but his dad convinced him to bite the bullet and get started.

COMMON IDIOM 6

Cat got your tongue?

The Cat's Got Your Tongue!

It means that you are at a loss for words. It may have come from a practice in ancient Egypt. The Egyptians worshipped several gods that were represented as cats. When someone was found to be a liar, his or her tongue was cut out as an offering to the cat god. Eventually, the phrase meant that someone was stumbling around for words, which sometimes happens when someone is lying!

A SAMPLE SENTENCE

"Did the cat get your tongue?" asked the teacher when the student didn't answer.

COMMON IDIOM 7

Caught red-handed

that's not mine!
VALERIAN

WHAT DOES IT MEAN?

It means you were caught doing something you weren't supposed to be doing. This idiom dates back to the country of Scotland in 1432. There was a law that someone could be charged with a crime if he killed an animal that wasn't his property. The law stated that the person had to be caught with evidence of blood splattered on his hands in order to be convicted and sentenced.

A SAMPLE SENTENCE

He tried to lie about stealing the gold, but he was caught red-handed.

COMMON IDIOM 8

Pull someone's leg

WHAT DOES IT MEAN?

It means to play a trick on someone. In London, in the 18th century, pairs of criminals would work together. One of them would trip the victim by pulling his leg or legs out from under him by using a cane or rope. While the victim was on the ground, the other criminal would pick his pockets. Today, it just means playing a trick or kidding someone.

A SAMPLE SENTENCE

He told me that I had won the lottery but he was only pulling my leg.

COMMON IDIOM 9
Turn a blind eye

WHAT DOES IT MEAN?

It means that you're choosing to ignore something. This idiom has a specific historical origin. In 1801, during a battle, Admiral Parker, who was the leader of the British forces, signaled Admiral Nelson to stop an attack on Danish ships. Admiral Horatio Nelson had an eye that was blinded, so he purposely raised a telescope to his blind eye and claimed to have never seen Admiral Parker's signal because he wanted to continue the battle. Nelson was successful and he took Parker's position. Parker had been disgraced because he wanted to end the battle.

ADMIRAL HORATIO NELSON

A SAMPLE SENTENCE

He knew that she was cheating on the exam, but he chose to turn a blind eye instead of reporting her.

COMMON IDIOM 10

Give the cold shoulder

WHAT DOES IT MEAN?

It means that you're disregarding someone or being unfriendly or aloof toward him or her. During the Middle Ages, welcome guests were given a hot meal such as roast beef that had just been prepared. If they received a cut of meat that was considered less than fresh, such as the cold shoulder of a piece of mutton, then this was a signal to them that they had worn out their welcome and should think about leaving.

A SAMPLE SENTENCE

Sue was nice to the new girl at her school, but most of the kids were giving the new kid the cold shoulder.

COMMON IDIOM II

Costs an arm and a Leg

WHAT DOES IT MEAN?

It means that something is very expensive. In the 18th century, portrait painters charged by whether just your head and shoulders were going to be painted in a portrait or whether your arms and legs were going to be included in a full-length portrait.

A SAMPLE SENTENCE

"I can't buy this dress for you," her mom said, "it costs an arm and a leg."

Quick Meaning:

It means something is easy.

Burn the Candle From Both Ends!

Quick Meaning:

It means going to bed late and get up early just to get the work done.

SUMMARY

An idiom is a phrase that means something completely different than what the words in the phrase actually mean. The English language is full of idioms, but we don't frequently think about where they came from. Many idioms have been around for centuries. Some have specific historical origins, but many of them have more than one possible origin so no one knows for sure where they came from. Idioms are always being added to the everyday language that people use to communicate.

The Apple of My Eye!

Quick Meaning:

It means the most favorite or cherished person.

Now that you've read about some common English idioms, you may want to read about a master of the English language in the Baby Professor book *Behind the Shadows of Romeo: A William Shakespeare Biography Book for Kids | Children's Biography Books.*

Visit
BABY PROFESSOR
EDUCATION KIDS
www.BabyProfessorBooks.com
to download Free Baby Professor eBooks
and view our catalog of new and exciting
Children's Books